CW00520920

Table of Content

About the Editor

Preface

Introduction

Childhood: Hard Inheritance

'Hands Up if you were adopted'

'Yellow Card'

On Remand in Horfield Lodge

'Red Card'

'Locked Up'

Newmarket Racing School and first winners!

Looking Back...Thinking forward

Journey's End

Healing Hearts

About the Editor

Professor Ray Kinsella has researched, taught and published extensively in healthcare economics. He has engaged closely with the work of Cuan Mhuire and Sr. Consilio, who suggested that he edit Anne's book.

Preface

Sister Consilio Fitzgerald SM. Founder and Guardian of Cuan Mhuire Residential Rehabilitation Community I am delighted to have been asked by Anne to write these few words of introduction to her book. From the very first time I met Anne I knew she was full of goodness and that she had a great heart.

She came to 'Cuan Mhuire' in Athy from a Hospital in Galway. She was in a lot of pain. Not alone physical pain – she was not in good shape and in need care and healing – she also needed healing from inside.

That kind of healing comes from a lived understanding that each one of us is made in the image and likeness of God. There is an infinite amount of goodness and giftedness within us. It could never be measured. When our addictions – and the suffering they bring us – are addressed in a positive way we can begin to understand, and embrace, the beautiful person that God has created us to be.

But there can be all kinds of difficulties, often relating to our childhood, that get in the way of our accepting this goodness and the gifts we have been given. The gifts we have been given are often covered up by a low self-worth, a lack of confidence and by fear. In Cuan Mhuire all of our residents are encouraged to first see their own goodness, because when they understand this goodness they can begin to understand and deal with the burdens they have been carrying. They can begin to develop their talents of all kinds.

These talents are there to be shared – with our families and especially those who are distressed. Anne has been blessed with an abundance of these creative gifts. She is a very gifted artist, just to take one example

Anne used to call herself 'Scotch Annie'! It was a great privilege having her come to us in Cuan Mhuire. Anne came and went and came back to us many times, as she was guided on the road towards recovery. That first time we prayed together we asked Our Blessed Lady to protect her, while she gradually came to understand her goodness, through all the ups and downs and byways of her journey towards recovery and her now very full and fulfilled life.

That first time, she told me that it was a young doctor in a hospital who had taken the trouble to really engage with her and to suggest that she come to Cuan Mhuire; and, even more importantly, to follow through by making the necessary arrangements. This shows how important a kind and positive word or suggestion can be – what a difference it can make to our lives.

The friendship of Anne and her husband Noel, and their two fine sons, has enriched my life and that of the Cuan Mhuire family. It is always good to welcome her when she is able to get away from London. Our former Residents are always welcome and many keep in touch, not just over the decades but across generations.

I was delighted when Anne told me that she was going to write a short book on her life. Every single person who recovers from addiction and embraces this recovery has their own unique story to tell. Anne's story – Anne book – is also unique.

She shows real honesty in describing her addiction to alcohol. She suffered a very great deal – she was hard on herself and often came to us in a bad way. She never looked for pity. And there was always a sense of fun and adventure about Anne which, even through the years of addiction about which she writes, she has never lost. That takes real strength of character. Behind the behaviours that arose from addiction there was always a truly good person, with real artistic gifts – and with just enormous courage. She was searching – without knowing it – for God's plan for her.

The turning point in Anne's life was the realization that if she was to overcome her addictions she needed something greater, more positive and more lasting than alcohol.. Love lasts. For Anne and Noel, having a family of their own was an expression of that love.

'Family' is a special part of Cuan Mhuire – part of an experience of belonging and of being acknowledged and valued. Having their own family, being graced with two children – her 'miracles', as Anne puts it so well – is what made the difference for her and for Noel. That is what motivated them to leave their addictions behind them.

Anne herself was blessed with parents who adopted her and who, in the fullest sense, loved her unconditionally through the pain and the turmoil that is the constant companion of addictions. That unconditional love was an extraordinary example and one Anne held on to in the hard times.

Anne and Noel had the great happiness of taking their two children, of whom they are so proud, back to her family home to thank her parents –her mother and father who never doubted her and whom she could share with her children.

Love is at the heart of Anne's story and it's my hope that many people will read it and reflect on all the insights that are there for those with an open mind and heart.

Introduction

By the time I was 12 years of age – that would have been about 1967 – I was drinking destructively. At 15, I was sent to an 'approved' school for almost 3 years. Then it got bad.

I spent upwards of 20 years living rough. Sometimes being admitted to hospitals of one kind or another, just long enough to get patched up and then get back on the drink again. Back to the world which, for alcoholics, is 'normal'. Not your 'normal', but ours: where we live out our lives by 'our' rules, not yours.

I was born in England in 1955. That's where I live now, in Epsom just outside of London. But, in between, I spent hard years – and had some good times – in Ireland. I went there first in the late 1970's; it would have been about 1978. I can't be sure of that date because I was in a complete blackout and just found myself there. There is no part of Ireland, north or south, that I haven't lived or drank in.

That is not as random as it seems. I had wanted to go to Ireland, to be there, because from the time I was a child I knew that it was a part of me. Having gone there, I only left for Scotland in 1986, having had a 'disagreement' about dole money with social services. It wasn't until the early 1990's that I went back to London where I now live with my husband Noel and our two children, enormously talented young men now building their own lives.

There were reasons why my life has turned out the way it has; both the bad parts and the good. Let me explain. When I finish a painting, it often surprises me the way the 'truth' of that painting emerges, almost as if it has a life of its own. My own life, in and out of addiction, has been like that. It has, just like any painting, been shaped by many influences: my struggles as a young adopted child to discover who 'I' was, alongside a fierce sense of rebellion during my teenage years and into my 20's that put me on a serious collision course with a normal life.

My addiction to alcohol was destructive. But, as I have said, there were reasons for that – forces at work. I haven't had a drink now for 25 years. I don't need it. Not as a crutch or something that, at least for a while, blots out the pain and alienation with which all alcoholics are familiar.

But I am no victim. I want to make that clear. It wasn't 'society' or bad parents or religion that made things turn out the way they did through those years. My parents were good, decent people who were always there for me – even with all of the grief that my rebelliousness caused them.

As for religion, the person who gave me the insight to see the unique value of my life and every other life is a Catholic nun. Sr. Consilio Fitzgerald welcomed me – drunk and in bits – at her rehabilitation centre in Ireland back in 1979. I remember it so well. Down the 10 years that followed, and they were difficult years, her complete acceptance of me as I was (and that the whole point) was my refuge and strength while living rough and living hard.

If you decide to read this book I want to tell you now that you won't like a lot of what you witness. Almost certainly, you won't like me as I was during those years. That's fine by me. I'm not out to shock. I'm not looking for your approval or sympathy. By my own lights, I'm an honest woman and what I have to say is the truth, warts and all, of what happened to me during those years of addiction to alcohol.

If you are reading this, bear in mind that sometimes the narrative of my life as it is set out in the book may sometimes jump from one event to another; there are gaps and what may seem to be inconsistencies. This is, quite simply, what 'blackouts' due to heavy drinking do to you. They

13

can disconnect time and make it difficult to connect events and people in a nice, tidy chronological order. But I have done my best, in this book of events and incidents and adventures during my years of addiction, to arrange things in a reasonable order.

This book is not about you or, for that matter, about me; it's for those of you who are struggling to understand, and to come to terms with, your addictions or that of a member of your family.

It's simply to give them a message of hope. Looking back, I now believe that if, as an alcoholic, you get to the stage of being able to remain sober for a while, you do become more in control of your emotional and physical feelings. It's not 'recovery' but it is a milestone on the road to recovery.

But you have to have a reason for doing it – a reason that is stronger than whatever it is that drives you to drink. And it has to be a reason that lasts. For me and for Noel, that reason was all about a family of our own – kids. Kids help you to get your head around what life is about, and what it can be about.

When you get to the point of being able to forgive yourself for your actions in the drink, your demons begin to disappear. It becomes easier to follow your own intuition without being influenced by other peoples' judgements of you.

That's important.

Today negative feelings of other people towards me – which once would have really got to me, at least for a while – pass straight through. It is as if these negative feelings, and the impulse to drink, have been removed by God. And I'm speaking as someone who did some crazy stuff and was diagnosed by psychiatrists and doctors as being a chronic alcoholic with liver damage and my chances of achieving – and maintaining – sobriety being slim to zero.

My life was changed with the help of special people. First, my parents, who adopted me. They had a hard time with me growing up and going off the rails. But at that time and even more so later when I came back into their lives again with young Sean and Paddy, they forgave me. That helped me to forgive myself. Their love of our two lads was the best thing ever for all of us.

All through my life, I was blessed to have met people who supported me unconditionally – in my deepest despair of addiction, on the long road to recovery and to my work today working as an artist in London. One of them I have mentioned. Sr. Consilio founded 'Cuan Mhuire' – Irish for 'Harbour of Mary', a detox and residential rehabilitation community for addicts in Athy, county Kildare in

1966. Funnily enough, it was at about this time, when I would have been 11 years old, that things were getting really bad for me – getting seriously out of control. She was the first person who was able to encourage me to love myself; just a little bit at first.

Then there was – and is – Noel my husband who I first met in the Simon refuge for the homeless. That was around the early to mid-1980's. Sr. Consilio and Noel have always been there for me. There were others who came into my life at certain times and made a real difference. Together with our two amazing boys and my dear friend Alison, they gave me the strength and courage to tell this story. Thanks also to Ray whom I met in Cuan Mhuire's new centre in Newry, which is amazing. He was visiting Sr. Consilio and had read my draft and helped me to organise, extend and edit it. My story may help others who are battling addictions; especially those who believe that they are by themselves, in a bad place. What I am saying to people in that position is – I've been there, been through it – there is always hope. Always.

Addiction can hit us all, men and women – fathers and mothers – and turn our lives upside down. It can be really tough on women because there are so many different sides to our lives. Young women are always vulnerable. And mothers give such a lot of themselves and their presence alone

make such an enormous difference to kid's lives –
that has been my experience. It's important to
understand that, however bad it gets God can turn
things around. He mostly does it though other
people.

Childhood: Hard Inheritance

I was adopted. I didn't know this as a little one. I know now that there can be an enormous amount of love when you are adopted. But being adopted is something that you grow into. It's not always easy. People who should know better can really mess with your head when they don't handle it positively and end up doing real damage. I was really blessed with my adoptive parents. Even so, there is stuff you may inherit without knowing it.

As a young child I always felt that there was something 'wrong' – maybe 'different' is a better word – with me. I didn't behave like other kids. If I was criticized for anything I felt I was under attack. For instance, I always liked to wear jeans and have short hair and didn't ever wear a dress unless I had to.

There were little things that instinctively felt different – like how, for example, I would pick up on some remark about poor people that seemed to me to be disrespectful and I would feel strongly about that – but I didn't understand why. Or even little things like how I held my knife and fork. I didn't know where these things were coming from but I did know how they set me apart, at least in my own head.

These were part of my hidden inheritance but I didn't know it and, not knowing it, I rebelled. I would shock people with what I came out with, like the way I really felt sympathy with ordinary people. Years and years later I said sorry to my Mother. She told me 'don't be sorry', that I would understand when my own children got a bit older; that she and my father always knew I would come back to them.

In my early school days I loved acting and poetry. This helped me to get out of this 'feeling different' space in my head and to kind of become the person I was acting out. My teacher was nice and always put me in the school play.

My adopted Dad worked in the Probate Registry in Downing Street. Sometimes he would take me to work. This was special. When I used to take part in poem recital (elocution) my Mum and me would go off to Lewis's shop and pick a dress for me to wear at competitions. My Mum would dress up and so would I.

Then again I hated wearing dresses. I was a proper tomboy. But I'd get up on the stage and recite my poem that I had learned off by heart with all the feeling I could. It was rare that I didn't come first. Mum had eight certificates she kept in her bottom drawer.

Later in childhood when Dad and my sister – who as a kid I never got on with – were showing off her O-Level and A-Level results, Mum would produce my certificates and show my trophy for tennis to visiting aunties and uncles.

My granny would sit me on her lap and talk french to me and call me her 'little flower'. She, like mum, had a soft spot for me and she liked me for being naughty. It made her laugh. When I remember these times, I remember she smelt of her lavender.

Then there was Aunt Joyce. She was rough and ready. She had young children herself and she understood them. She wasn't really my aunt. She was a friend of my mum's from church and was in fact my godmother. She was so nice and practical and good that we just called her Aunt Joyce.

She would fill me with confidence. I would tell her about my sister and some of the things we would argue about. She would tell me to take no notice of her, that sometimes girls might only be mean to me because they were jealous. 'You are such a good girl' she would say and sometimes my sister wasn't. Thinking back, she was probably kind to my sister too – but I really needed her understanding at that time. I was a kid. She was my Godmother. And she never ever forgot my birthday

What she said about me being a 'good one' was music to my ears; me, 'the good one'. She also told me I was beautiful and she loved me just as much as her own children. I would go and stay with her during the holidays. She lived in Winchester where her husband Bill was a pharmacist. His shop, with all the coloured bottles, was fascinating for any child.

He loved my drawings and loved me coming to stay. Aunt Joyce would tell me stories, which I loved. She wrote to me right through all of my drinking years. When I met Sr. Consilio first she reminded me of Aunt Joyce and I think that's why we got on so well, right from the very start.

Back to my sister. My sister was a real lady and took pride in her appearance. It was made clear to me that, in her opinion, I didn't have a good 'look' about me. This made me rebel even more and, so, for example, my clothes became more extreme. She was also brainy and did well at school and never once gave cheek or trouble.

My poor Mum was always stuck in the middle. She would often burst into tears when my sister would verbally attack me and sometimes say stuff she shouldn't. I would call her names. Dad would take her side and my poor Mum would try to stick up for me but the others would be too strong verbally and Mum would cry.

That would really upset me. I would call the two of them all the bastards under the sun. They would say it was my fault that Mum was upset. I hated them at this early stage, as a little one. Not my Mum, though – she was, in my eyes, an angel, who always saw the best in people. I loved her. She asked me things like, did I like flowers and animals and we'd talk for ages. When I think of my early childhood memories they are happy ones. Today, I know that I was very lucky to have a Mum and Dad at all. Even now when I smell fire I think of my childhood and it's always a nice warm feeling inside.

I remember the times my Dad took me to work with him in the Probate Registry, an old Victorian wood room with panels and old oil paintings of men and I had no notion of who they were. But he would tell me all about them and, also, how he worked in Downing Street after the war.

Once a week my granddad (my adopted dad's father) would visit us from Kenley in London, where he lived with my aunt, a school teacher. He would take me for walks sometimes and he would get me a bar of chocolate out of a vending machine. If I walked a long way we would talk for hours. Having been a soldier in the First World War he was never short of stories, from his childhood in Galway to how he contracted malaria in Kenya.

My granddad was lovely, really lovely. Looking back I remember how he had snow white hair and smelt of eau de cologne; he was kind and witty and spent time with me. He was a lovely granddad and he adored Mum. So I was lucky really. Adoption – now there is a thing. It's complicated. Some children don't get adopted and spend their lives in and out of care. This doesn't give you a strong foundation in life as being a rounded human being.

Everyone needs a Mum and Dad. Even if you go astray later in life, you won't forget what it takes to live a right life, and what it takes to be good parents when you are settled again and you have overcome your demons.

But what I'm talking about is the whole matter of adoption and young kids understanding what it actually means. Parents – a mother and a father – can only do so much. There are always other influences at work. But my parents loved me through it all – and that's the best thing you can say about parents.

'Hands Up if you were adopted'

I was about six when we moved from Purley to Bristol. Dad got a promotion and became Head Registrar at Bristol Probate Registry office. My sister and I changed schools and went to a convent, St Ursula's Bristol. Our new home was in Westbury-on-Trym, Bristol.

I liked it there. Shortly after we arrived I went off on my bike to explore and I ended up visiting some horses in a field. I always wanted riding lessons but this wasn't possible because my Mum and Dad were already paying private fees for me and my sister to give us the best start in life at a good school.

My sister, fair play to her, took full advantage and worked hard. But I nearly had to be tied to a chair by my Dad, to do any homework at all. I hated school; the teachers didn't like me and singled me out. So I was outside the headmistress' office more times than I was in class. I think my sister would have liked me to be a bit like her but I was doing my best to say, and do, the very opposite to her.

And then something happened that changed my life. One day a teacher said in class: 'hands up all those who are adopted'. To this day, I don't know why she asked that question. Maybe there was a reason; maybe she as looking for our birth certificates. But out of the blue she asked that very question. I was only little at the time – I remember my rocking horse in my room – so I could only have been about six or so. I looked around the room and I expected everyone to have their hands up. My mum had always told me that being adopted was good; she would, for example, talk to me about my teddy bear who she said was also adopted. So adoption had never been an issue for me. But I was suddenly devastated when I saw that I was the only one in the class with my hand up. The next day I was terrorised by a girl who said my Mother had 'not wanted me'. I was suddenly completely confused. I ran home and told my Mum.

I remember her telling me: 'we chose you out of many babies; you were the special one we chose. Your real Mum couldn't take care of you so we said we would and you are ours forever and ever'. This was really wise of her and it's the way she had always been with me. But the whole episode really shook me and my confidence and cast a long shadow into my future.

My sister didn't do anything wrong at school and very quickly became a school prefect. She was seven years older than me but, in my opinion at the time, she was brainwashed: she always thought before she opened her mouth. Her views weren't right, in my mind. She seemed to me, at that time, to think she was above poor people and didn't have much time for anyone who wasn't white, middleclass and clever. That was a kid's way of thinking – but I was a kid. So, I thought of her as being narrow minded. My sister wanted to become a teacher. I did a lot of painting and I wanted to be an artist. I also wanted to be singer, my voice was husky –although not everyone's cup of tea.

But still I found joining in and making friends difficult. I did want to play sports – part of being a tomboy – and I was good them. When I think of my own lads today and what they are achieving in sports I would like to think that they inherited something of that from me. But because my school work and behaviour weren't good, I often wasn't picked for the team – this made me resentful.

I liked geography, drawing maps and taking ages to do them – and they were quite good! Quite good? In my mind they were really good, as I had done them free hand while all the rest of the class traced them. But I didn't spend much time on the written work, as I had no interest it.

I loved working class people, and they seemed to think like me. Maybe this was something in my inheritance – maybe there was some kind of instinct at the root of how I felt, even before the whole issue of 'adoption' came up at school. Anyway, my best friend Sally Corrigan had Irish parents (I didn't know then that my biological dad was from Dublin). Sally was the nicest, funniest, craziest and, most important, the naughtiest rebel I had ever met.

The only thing I wanted to do was to get expelled from the convent and go to the ordinary school, Laurence Weston for Boys and Girls – and I did, later on. The days dragged on and on at St Ursula's. I became aware of an emptiness inside me – who was I? Where did I come from? Was this feeling of 'not belonging' and most people trying to change me – was it because I was adopted? I was convinced it was, so I continued to rebel.

There were a number of reasons for this. In part, it was that feeling I had since I was a small kid of being 'different'. That whole experience of coming face to face with what some of the other kids thought – in fact, they knew nothing – about what adoption really meant. And there was there was the feeling of being compared unfavourably with my sister, of falling short of what she was all about even though I knew that I had my own abilities – things like art that to which I really felt attracted.

I was about 10 at this stage. Every day there seemed to be arguments which made me more rebellious. There were little things that I did, like saying straight out things I felt were not reality. This went against me.

I would be told: 'you were given an education the same as your sister. You were given every chance going to be a good human being – but you are never going to amount to anything. Artists don't make money so you need proper qualifications'. But because I was a bit behind at school, they kept be down a class each year. I found adding up and spelling hard. Trying to concentrate didn't help, there was just a blockage. All of this only added to my frustration making me want to push back at it by rebelling.

If I did something wrong, like stay out late or steal sweets from the shop, I would get the sharp end of my Dad's tongue. Christine never did. I felt they favoured her, even though she was quite often the one to blame for my answering back at meal times. I hated her at this time. It was so easy for her to stay out of trouble and she knew just when to button her mouth. It was probably only a matter of time before something happened.

The Gallops' one of my recent paintings

'Bad Girl'

One day, Sally announced to me she was moving to what we called 'the naughty school', Laurence Weston. This shook me since she was my really best friend and I didn't have too many friends! With all the pressures I had inside, I felt I had to act fast to get expelled because she was going in four weeks. I was already in constant trouble with the Headmistress at St Ursula's High School, so I thought that another couple of episodes of bad behaviour wouldn't be a problem.

Sr. Cecilia was the headmistress at that time. She would just know things. Sometimes when I would go to the cloakroom and be very bold running around, she would just know what I was up to. But she could also say the right kind of 'good things' to get kids to behave. She would tell me stop 'horseplay', that my parents wanted me to be 'sensible' and 'ladylike'.

She was a good woman and nun and I really liked her. Even though, as a result of all of my efforts, she did expel me from school, I always had respect for Sr. Cecilia. Looking back now, I thought St Ursula's was great but, really, for all the wrong reasons. I carried on disrupting the class until I was finally expelled – I didn't go to school most days anyway.

I would often go to Sally's house after school. My poor Mum wouldn't know where I was. Sometimes I forgot to ring and tell her I was at Sally's house. Sally and I got on so well but she didn't get on well with my sister. Sally was an amazing artist, a bit of a hippy and her mum and dad took no notice of me around the place. They had a very 'modern' outlook on life and they let Sally be herself and dress how she wanted. They never criticised anyone who was 'a bit hippy'.

This was the late 1960's and there were a lot of young people who were rebels like me around. Bob Dylan music rang through Sally's house. Her own paintings were on the wall. I loved it all – it was my haven. My favourite music was Pink Floyd – and still is to this day.

Sally was clever and although she was naughty she helped me not to get caught when I was getting up to being bold. We were about the same age – thirteen – and we went everywhere together. She loved Jimmy Hendrix and Janice Joplin was her favourite singer.

One day she said something that was to totally change my feeling of being a bit of a follower and who was just being influenced by song lyrics. It was August 1970 – we were coming up to 15. There was a massive pop concert planned for the Isle of Wight – biggest ever, everyone was playing. We had talked for hours about how we could get there and actually see Jimmy Hendrix on stage. We could already draw his face really well.

We never got to the concert; we were just talking about it, the way girls do. But what was so important to me was that Sally told me something that gave me great confidence. She said that I could sing just like Janice Joplin. Well, that was the best compliment anyone could have given me at that time

– a time when I was really impressionable and one I would never forget. It shows you how important the good word can be – especially to a kid.

But, of course, when I started at Laurence Weston School, Sally and I were separated almost straight away. I was put in a different class. But it wasn't long before I found some more outrageous 'friends' who would scoot off to the nearest park to avoid school.

And it was then I discovered my love of alcohol – my hard inheritance. My adopted Mum and Dad hardly drank any alcohol, only at Christmas. So I would take gin or vodka, pour it into a plastic pop bottle and water down what was left. If I took whiskey, I would get water and dip a teabag in it and then put the water in the original bottle so it looked like whiskey. Most of the time no-one noticed. Dad would just go and buy another saying that it had been there a long time and must have fermented.

Sometimes at my old school, you could have a fag in the girls' loo. But in this school they were smoking weed, so that was a big jump for me. We would share a joint at break time and I would go and shop lift make-up to be able to pay for fags and drink. I wasn't really made on smoking dope, it made me mellow – but what I wanted was something to make me a bit drunk.

Now I could sing like Janice Joplin, dance, drink any bloke under the table and was, according to people I asked for an honest opinion, very good looking – to my surprise. So I was feeling a lot more confident about myself; no-one before this had told me I was nice looking. Mum and Dad would never say my sister was, or wasn't, nice to look at – just that she looked very nice in her clothes.

'Yellow Card'

I wasn't even 15 years of age. But I was getting into alcohol. With drink, I felt I could achieve anything. By now my sister had disowned me altogether. If I bumped into her in the street, she would pretend she didn't know me, so my friends and I would terrorise her. I was full of self-belief. Her opinion didn't hurt me anymore. I sometimes pretended to go to school for peace sake, but I would hide my jeans, shoes and t-shirt in a bush, change clothes and leave my school stuff in the bush.

Sometimes I would get drunk and I wouldn't remember where I'd hidden my uniform, so I would lie to Mum and she would have to get another one. My poor Mum also had to open the door at all times of the night to let me in, as my Dad wouldn't. I don't blame him – he didn't know what to do.

I had gone completely off the rails. I would sit on the stairs and listen to them trying to figure out what to do with me and maybe to send me away. I would come down stairs and tell them I'd heard them say they were gonna give me away, 'like my first Mum did'. My poor Mum would plead with me to listen to them; she would tell me that they both loved me very much but didn't know what to do about my stealing, drinking and not going to school. My sister would join in and say I was a horrible sister who didn't deserve Mum and Dad. I told her she was ugly and I hated her – poor Christine with mousey hair, and a member of the Young Conservatives (a bit of a loser I thought).

I was already getting involved with anarchists and all different walks of life. One friend who I loved to bits was a heroin addict; she was 20 and already had two kids and used to shoot up heroin in from of them. This stayed in my head. It scared me as sometimes she would inject between her toes to get a vein that wasn't broke down. As soon as everybody got really out of it I'd go out hunting for drink. I wouldn't go near the needle ever; it scared me, especially when I heard she had died. She was found in some bushes overdosed in the garden. Poor girl, she was such a good person but she was so addicted to heroin nothing mattered but the next fix.

On Remand in Horfield Lodge

Around this time I was caught shop lifting drink. But because I wasn't quite 15 years I was still legally meant to be at school. So the Juvenile Court sent me to The Horfield Lodge remand home for 3 weeks. I was a bit nervous so I just sat in a corner, away from the more confident residents and drew pictures.

One girl – and the most popular girl – was the ring leader of the whole group; she had been on the game for some pimp in Bristol. She was nice and we were allowed to listen to music in the evening .Everyone would get up and have a dance. We would start them off, and we would always play Michael Jackson singing 'Billy Jean'! To this day, he remains my absolutely favourite artist. They all said I could dance really well! So my few weeks on remand passed quickly and I was released. I would miss my new found friends but, I thought, it would mean freedom at last. But not for long!

'Red Card'

My bad behaviour got worse. I'd stay out all night and if I staggered home drunk I didn't even ring the bell and would just sleep in the shed in our garden. Sometimes Mum would see the shed door open and when Dad had gone off to the office to work, she would come down the garden path and bring me up the house for a bath and change of clothes. I always remember we all had linen white sheets; they were always crisp and it was lovely getting into a clean bed. Sometimes I'd be gone for two or three days. I was just 15 years old at the time. Mum and Dad were at their wits end. Mum had to take valium – her nerves were so bad, with Christine and Dad against me day-in day-out and her trying so hard to let me know she still loved me. I knew that I had to change before it was too late – easy to say.

One week they went away. I broke into their house; I say 'their' because I was really kind of detached from home by that stage, what with staying out until all hours and not bothering about the effect it was having on them. They told me that the house wasn't a hotel – that it was a home, and that if I wanted to stay I could get a job and make some kind of contribution.

I'm sure they were just trying to teach me about respect.

But I wasn't listening. They had gone away for a week without even telling me. How dare they! The thing is that I wasn't even around for them to tell me they were going away for a break. I was just a kid with a messed-up head and resentful.

So I broke in through the French windows. This time I took the drink without diluting it – I was thinking, 'how could they go on holiday with Christine and leave me alone?' A neighbour had heard the glass smash and called the police. I was arrested and charged with being beyond parent's control. Without going to court, I was taken by the police to Horfield Lodge and went to court four days later. My Mum and Dad could do nothing for me this time. My lovely Mum had to hold back the tears as they led me away. I was gutted – there were no more chances; this was it: I got two years eight months in so-called state 'Approved School'.

I burst into tears. I was getting separated from those two people that I adored with all my heart, but it was too late and I was now in the hands of the Court for being beyond parent's control. I was fifteen years old and I would be released when I was 18, and not before.

Suddenly, I became the vulnerable child again. The 'hard' image slipped away. I was 'Anne' again. I felt like I was having a nervous breakdown. My behaviour in school, and after I had been expelled, was bad. But I missed my mum and dad so much.

'Locked Up'

As far as the law was concerned , I was now those few months older than when I was in Horfield Lodge a few months earlier for shoplifting. I had crossed over the line. I was taken to the State 'Approved School called 'St Joseph's by the police. It was quite a drive, to near Chippenham and then down a long driveway. At the end of the driveway was a large, old looking, building. A nun came to the door, shook my hand and led me through a long shiny corridor with stone walls and heavy doors.

A few of the doors had bars on them and I asked the nun what they were for – she said they were the 'lock-up' – where you go if you don't behave. I shuddered and told myself that I would definitely avoid going in there. There was a musky smell like an old cellar and I was led into the room where a small stone faced nun stood. As I entered, the nun who took me there, and who was nice, left and shut the door behind her.

She said 'I am Sr. Eugene and you have been sent to me by the Courts to change your ways'. I said nothing. I went into my 'I don't hear you bitch' mode but what she spat out at me was horrible. I wouldn't listen to this stuff. I wouldn't cry to spite her. She rang a bell and like a little dog the nun who took me there came back in and led me off to meet my House

Sister, Sr. Genevieve. She wasn't bad, in fairness, and said she was the one to come to if I needed anything.

The girls slept in long dormitories with a faint light. A nun would check on us through the night. She was like a ghost in the distance, with her long white robes.

All the girls there were all able to fight, so I didn't get too mouthy with anyone. I was scared of what might happen. But I knew I had to learn to fight, or I'd have two years of living hell! One girl in particular was a bully. She would kick girls under the table and take their pudding and eat it. I used to look at her but I hadn't plucked up enough courage to respond. But I said to myself she was 'the one'. The girls called her 'Big Bad Beatrice'. She continued to look at me funny.

Sometimes Mum would send me a parcel. The other girls got parcels from their parents too. One day Beatrice took some shampoo that Mum had sent to me. But I still said nothing.

I made one friend, Rosalyn; tall, skinny, funny, she liked hippies, and she loved my drawings. There was another friend, Angie who was a 'Hells Angel'. It was her that told me 'You have to fight that Beatrice'. She told me: 'She thinks she is bad.

41

We don't let her away with nothing – you mustn't either or she will get worse'. I said 'Okay, I will, but not yet'. I hadn't plucked up enough courage yet. I cried a lot when I thought of my Mum and Dad, but never in front of anyone.

One day that same girl threw a scrubbing brush at my head. I did nothing until she said something disrespectful about my Mum. I asked her 'what did you say bitch?' I don't know where it came from but I won't forget her reply: 'get ready to die'. I went up to her, my arms down, and then let one fist fly straight into her fat gut; down she went, and then got up and ran up the corridor, nearly slipping on the soap. A friend was doing 'look-out' for me. She pissed herself laughing and ran to the common room to tell everyone that the new one, Anne, beat the shit out of 'Big Bad Beatrice'. She exaggerated it, of course. But it had the desired effect; everyone left me alone after that, peace at last. I did get in a few fights after that and was thrown in the 'lock-up'. But my mates would slide a fag under the door and some matches. Time passed quickly; I'd just sleep most of the time.

I was two years there when they did a 'School Play', Oliver Twist. The Drama teacher – who also taught art, which I enjoyed – gave me one of leading roles, as Fagan. I practiced for a month: all the words and actions of Fagan ('you've got to pick a pocket or two'), the funny walk, the beard and a big nose. I looked the picture of Ron Moody playing the part. As the day of the play drew near we all could hardly wait for the excitement. Mum and Dad were thrilled with my acting and I got a standing ovation.

A woman approached my Mum and asked her when I left St Joseph's would she please contact her and gave her a phone number. She worked at the Old Vic in London and said my performance as Fagan was sensational. I never did follow-up, but the reaction to my acting was great and that was a real positive me for me, especially at that time.

Finally, it was over. It was about 4 pm and Sr. Genieve (incidentally, a big Jim Reeves Country and Western fan) came to find me and tell me: 'Your mother and Father are here for you'. A lot of people came by to say they would miss me. In fact, I did meet some of them months and even years later. I might be hanging around St Pauls with some student friends and I'd occasionally see one of the girls 'on the game' and they would wave to me. Tough on them.

But on that special afternoon I couldn't wait to get away – my mum and dad were waiting for me. They had come to visit every four weeks through my sentence – never missed a week. So, of course, they were there right on time and they had 10 fags for me, bless them. I went home with them. My sister wasn't at home. She was at Hull University where she was graduating in six months. But I had headed off on my travels by that time.

Probation and why it didn't work for me

I was, in fact, released into a work hostel where I stayed at night and worked in a shop in Bath during the day. This was part of the conditions of my release. It lasted for two months until my 18th birthday. Occasionally student friends would come into the shop and try on a coat or whatever. I would sometimes take the alarm off whatever they had chosen and they'd walk out with it.

I always had fags. But I didn't drink alcohol again until I was out of the Hostel. I knew that if I blew my stay in the hostel they could say I hadn't reformed and I would go straight to Borstal, which is the same as jail. I met the probation officer right at the start of my release. He told me I couldn't stay out late at night – that I must be back at 10pm. Most people I knew were actually only going out at that time. I knew this probation thing wouldn't last. It didn't.

On the run – new place, new name

Once I left the hostel, I spent most of my time with squatters in Clifton. It was close by home. My mum and dad were conscious that I was now 18, that I had grown up a lot. They weren't worried about me so much – but they would have liked for me to get a job, a flat and a life. I didn't want them to be distressed about me coming and going – so I stayed with my friends in squats.

My friends liked my paintings and loved me singing with them when they were jamming with their band – drummer, bass guitar, lead guitar. All of the equipment they got from selling weed. Sometimes we would get a gig at a pub and off we'd go. I sang the blues. That was my thing. After that we got work in clubs. I normally didn't get paid – just free drink but that suited me.

I now moved around, staying with squatters. I stayed with some anarchists who went to marches and demonstration all the time: gay rights, black rights, feminist rights and any organisation that was anti-police. I didn't have any good relationships with boys. I often got beaten up – they only wanted to use me and I just didn't want to go there. This made it difficult to have a relationship with boys – and then there was the drink. So boys were only good mates if they were gay.

46

I drew the dole every week and moved to different towns 'signing on' under different names. Sometimes in the summer I would head for the seaside. I loved the sea and I would sleep in caves with a blanket. Then I'd head for somewhere else; no place in particular, wherever I'd end up.

A little Time in Holloway

I was already wanted for 'breach of probation' when the police caught me for shoplifting. I had to go back to court for the shoplifting offense and they put me in Holloway, the women's Prison. I wasn't much bothered at this stage like I had been when I was put in the 'Approved School'. I was frightened of no-one, and was well able to fight now! So no-one even looked sideways at me – they thought I was hard. All an act – deep down, I was just Anne.

When I got out of Holloway I agreed to go and stay at a probation hostel in Bristol. That was okay, as I was to appear in Bristol magistrates Court in a week's time anyway. I drew the dole with a letter from the hostel. I was drinking but I did get into the hostel on time for a few days. I didn't have enough money for drink and I had to make do with methylated spirits – meth's – which can be used for paint-stripping.

I had a terrible bender with drink – the result of mixing wine and meth's. I was due to appear in court in just a day or two later. I went to a doctor to get some valium; in the past I had taken some of my Mum's and I knew they stopped the shakes. But the doctor wouldn't give me any. She said she thought I was becoming cross-addicted, dependent on valium as well as on drink.

The DT's and what they do to You

So I headed back for the hostel. I had
nowhere else to go. I was shaking and sweating and I
knew I was going into the DT's – which are part of
the serious side-effects when you stop drinking
without being properly detoxed.

When you are a serious alcoholic you may
hear voices and people talking to you in your head;
you see things crawling on your skin and you
actually feel them as well. I was in bad shape. I went
into the shower to wash these things off my skin and
to escape the voices in my head – voices which I
thought were actually moving the shower curtain. I
was aware of a terrible presence of evil. This was
scary; it was much more than imagining things
caused by drink. I was afraid for my mind, for 'me',
Anne. The voices were horrid and nasty, telling me
to harm myself. I couldn't get the shadows on the
ceiling to stop moving.

I couldn't tell what was real. I knew I was
sick but it was getting more intense – I was going to
die. I was conscious of this evil because I was so
vulnerable. Don't ever let them tell you that the devil
is not real. The devil can do a lot when drugs or drink
really sap you of life and of your will. This was the
first time I had experienced this evil. I was being

pushed to end it; I just remember thinking and calling out: 'help me, God', as I leaped out of a second story window. When I woke up, I was in hospital in intensive care; on a drip, bandaged with my leg up in the air in plaster. 'What happened?' I asked, 'I thought I'd been hit by a car'. The doctor then told me that I had tried to kill myself. But I knew I hadn't – I knew it was the effects of the unsupervised withdrawal of drink. The doctor told me 'You have two steel pins holding your leg together, you have a broken nose, you had major plastic surgery on your face – but the plastic surgeon has done a good job and you should be fine'.

When the swelling went down Mum and Dad came to see me. They just never gave up on me – imagine how they felt? I couldn't wait to get discharged. A week later I had stopped losing brain fluid and I was given crutches and I went to my friend Monica and from there I went to the Magistrates Court.

Decent Judge

The case was read out loud and I hobbled up to the steps. 'Stay where you are Anne' said the judge. She went on to say: 'Now, in spite of the fact Anne has committed crimes and broke the law, she is sorry. I think Anne has suffered enough. Her injuries are beyond belief. I have to give her a chance. Therefore, I release you to make a new start'. She was a star. I said 'Thank you, Judge. I will do my best and go to AA'.

Off I went. My anarchist friends were in court and cheered at the decision of the judge – decent woman. Monica my lovely friend from Sweden took me home to her flat and we had a meal of brown rice and brown bread. She told me she was going to London and asked me would I come with her. I jumped at the chance. She was doing a feminist exhibition of her painting and asked me would I like to put two of my oil paintings alongside hers.

Monica and Missing out on the Edinburgh Festival

I only drank a small amount of cider with Monica and her husband. I threw away the crutch, as I could walk better without it, but Monica brought it along for me just in case. Monica drove one of those hippy vans with flowers on the side of it. She was full of wisdom, like an earth mother and she could see so much meaning in my paintings that I sometimes couldn't see. Off we went to London and stayed at a lesbians' squat. They were friendly and didn't care that I was straight – they could sense I passed no judgement.

Me and Monica headed for the art exhibition the next day. It was a big gallery and her paintings had arrived a week before and were already hanging up on the wall. She got two hooks and hung mine up. She had let me use her oils and brushes; it had kept me busy when my body was healing from the effects of the fall.

After people were shown Monica's work she showed them mine and introduced me as an artist and blues singer. I was thrilled. She sold both of my paintings for £50 each. I was delighted at the first of what was to be many art exhibitions.

Monica had arranged for me to sing at the Edinburgh festival. But I wasn't in the mood for going off to Edinburgh and didn't think I was good enough to sing there. Instead, I was all for going back on the drink and heading for Ireland. I hadn't been there before but always loved the Irish. It was, as I was to discover, a part of my heritage, my birth father being from Dublin.

So I went toward the motorway and flagged down a lorry. As usual, I carried a knife in case a lorry driver tried anything. In fact, most of the men were good people with families of their own and they picked me up just to keep me safe. They warned me of the dangers of hitch hiking on my own. They were right, and I had a few near misses – but with drink down me, I didn't have an ounce of sense.

Off to Ireland

I got to Liverpool and found a hostel and signed on. I went to social services and told them a pack of lies about how I had family in Ireland and my husband had beaten me up in Bristol and I had to get away. I showed them my 'war wounds' – the large scar on my head and leg from my fall.

So, they believed me and paid my ticket on the ferry. I was 19 and I was back drinking. I can't remember getting on, or off, the ferry or even arriving in Dublin. But I woke up from a blackout in Mullingar in a 'County Home' – a kind of safety net for indigents with nowhere else to go – and with no notion of how I got there.

The next day I hitch hiked to Dublin and got into the 'Regina Coeli' (Queen of Heaven) hostel for women. This was opposite the 'Morning Star' Hostel for men. Both of these were well-known places of refuge opened by the Legion of Mary. The Regina Coeli cared for and looked after women. Next day I asked one of the men coming out of the Morning Star. – who turned out to be a road man — where I could get a change of clothes and he told me the St Vincent de Paul would help me, and they did. I got a letter from the Regina Coeli and headed for the 'Assistance Man' to get money.

Off with me for Cork, then next Waterford, Galway, Connemara, Kerry, Sligo, Derry, Belfast and Dundalk. I was stopping off in Hostels. Sometimes I would stay in psychiatric hospitals, just to get a few days rest – time out from the effects of the road and the drink. This went on for a year or so. I was getting bad again with the drink and the kind of life that would be hard on anyone. When I got to Galway I signed myself into a hospital, knowing that I was close to the point of bad withdrawals and the DT's.

I had been travelling around a lot and needed a rest. So, when the Doctor came to turn down my drip of Heminevrin for withdrawal he told me about a nun from Kerry who took in alcoholic men and women and helped get them off the booze; no pressure, as long as it takes. I agreed. 'I'll make a call, so' he said. And so he did.

A few days later he told me he had arranged for someone to drive me to Athy, County Kildare to 'Cuan Mhuire' to meet this nun from Kerry. Her name was Sr. Consilio and she changed my whole life.

Meeting Sister Consilio

A taxi arrived at the hospital to take me to Cuan Mhuire Athy Co. Kildare where Sr Consilio, the nun who the doctor had told me about and who said she would welcome me, was based.

But I still had to have another drink so I told the taxi to drop me off in the town of Athy, not far from Cuan Mhuire. I got a bottle of wine and headed off to drink it. Then I went to a pub got into a fight, and after that again I headed for the Cuan Mhuire house – which was built on a farm – with the Gardaí (police) driving me. I walked down the long driveway and to reception. I had cut my head and fell over something. So, when I walked in I was a bit rough and quite drunk.The man on the desk paged Sr. Consilio to come to reception. She hurried to me, smiled and said she was glad I had got there. That was all that mattered. I liked her straight away. She invited me to stay there for a while and to get well again.

Sister Consilio

I so remember her taking my hand in hers and telling me 'I can see you have a lot of heart Anne, and I see an awful lot of good in you'. I told her about my life and she seemed to really feel all the pain I had experienced, and that was in me.

She asked me to say one prayer to Our Lady for having brought me to 'Cuan Mhuire', which means 'Harbour of Mary'—and what a journey I had been on. I wanted a fag first. She understood that and said she would get me some fags shortly. She then took and held my hand and, from that day, asked Our Lady to come to my protection.

Noel's Family

I felt at peace, as if something extraordinary – something I had never experienced before – had passed through me. I knew then for certain sure that, whatever happened, it would be all right – that the story would have a happy ending. But there were still hard miles to travel.

Sr. Consilio is so special; she loves helping people with addiction because God has given her a gift. She has saved the lives of not just me but of so many suffering alcoholics, drug addicts and gambling addicts, working with all these specialised medics and councillors and also with kind volunteers, many of whom had been through addictions themselves. She not only gets them sober but also helps them through her aftercare and works with their families to sort out their lives.

I got restless and left Cuan Mhuire. But I knew it was a place I would return to one day. In fact, I can back there quite a few times on my road to sobriety. Sr. always says that there is a time for everything and not to feel bad if this is not your time; the important thing is to know you are welcome when you come back because then might be the right time. In the meantime, I had learned just what unconditional love really means.

I headed for Donegal and then Newry. I was very drunk one day and wandered into the wrong area for an obvious drunk Catholic – that was the way things were back then – and was pulled into a car by two men. I thought I was going to be lifted for shop lifting or something. But they were quite obviously telling the truth when they told me who they actually were. They dropped me back in Newry; back where they, and I, knew was safe – lucky for me.

I wasn't so lucky when, about a year before I met Noel, I ran into this man who I drank with. He was, I thought, a friend! But one day he told me if I walked away from him, he would kill me. I was staying at a hostel and he didn't want me to go back there. All I remember after that is a sharp thud on the back of my head.

I woke up in hospital on a drip of hemineverin for alcohol withdrawal. They asked me did I want to see how my face was – I had been beaten to a pulp, the nurse told me. Both my cheek bones were broken and my nose, again. I had got a bang; my mouth was so swollen and I had a tooth knocked out. They never did find my attacker but he had left me to die!

Changing Identity

Part of the whole thing about being addicted and on the road has to do with identity. The first time I changed my name I was just out of State 'Approved School'. I figured I was on my own, no-one wanted to know me and I thought I don't want to know them either. So I gave myself a new name – 'Scotch Annie'. It seemed as good a reason as any for a celebration for someone with a new identity and a new name, 'Anne Doherty'.

I had already signed on under my real name successfully, drew my money and went to Cardiff. I couldn't use my own name in Cardiff so I used my new name, Anne Doherty. I signed on the next day after spending the night in a hostel and getting a letter from the hostel to apply for a medical card and proof of residence.

Within three weeks I had received a medical card in the name of Doherty and my back money. I didn't pay the hostel and I didn't want to outstay my welcome. I had one more stop to make under my real name, as I had a giro waiting for me. I picked up the giro, cashed it and I headed for Liverpool.

I now had my two medical cards, one in my own name and one in my new name.

I arrived in Liverpool in the early morning having hitched a couple of lifts from lorry stops. I had a few pounds down my sock and managed to find myself an 'early house' – where you could get drink before the pubs opened and head for the park benches.

The park bench was the one place you would always find someone who would let you know all the local haunts, such as convents, local priests, vicars, ministers, any local St. Vincent de Paul or any other charitable organisations. You could find out from someone which of the off-licences were easy pickings. They would also let you know any hostels in the area and what dole office would cover that hostel.

Now that I had two ID's I would book myself into another hostel in a different area and draw the dole. This was all fine except when I had too much drink taken. Then there was always the danger of turning up at the wrong dole office, with the wrong ID. I would always sense when this had happened because they would send me to sit down and then call me to a different window. When that happened, I knew that it was time to leave. I then headed for the off licence, thinking about how I messed up the claims.

There was one particular time – I'd gone back to the off licence and on out to the park bench. The next thing I remember was when I woke up in a strange place – Mullingar. This was just another blackout, when you would just lose track of time and events, wake up and not know where you were or how you got there.

The Assistance Man

At one time in Ireland, as long as you had an address – but no proof of living at the address, maybe living in a caravan or tent – you were entitled to money to live. To get it, you had to apply to the 'Assistance Man'.

One time when I was in Limerick I went to the 'Assistance Man' and gave my address as a tent in a field. He wasn't convinced so I had to show him and he agreed to come with me. I had, in fact, been sleeping in a hay barn in a field and I had picked that as my address. I took him down the road to the gate and he had to climb over it, which took him a while. It was winter time and it was very wet and very mucky. As he stepped off the gate in his fine new suit and new shoes he nearly went to his knees in muck.

I will always remember the way looked at me. I think he had tears in his eyes and he said 'I've gone far enough'. He gave me £35.65 and told me not to bother him anymore. I thanked him and took the money. He left and walked towards his office.

But of course there was no tent. The only thing that was bothering me as I watched him walk down the road was the way he kept looking at his shoes and trousers. I was waiting to get to the nearest off licence. I found one, got my drink and got on the road to hitch a lift to wherever was my next destination.

Noel comes into my Life

I headed for Dundalk and stayed for the night at the Simon Community's Hostel for the homeless who helped the homeless with a bed and a meal for a night.. I was going to sign-on on Monday and this was Saturday evening. It was a men only hostel, but Clare Cody always let me in – she was my friend and I liked her a lot. So, I went to bed downstairs and two men came in later, staggered past me. One man said 'I nearly trod on you, what are you doing sleeping on the floor, are you alright?'; 'Yes', I said; 'Okay I'm off to bed, see you in the morning, there's my bed you can have it if you want, I'll sleep here' he said. 'No, it's okay', I told him. The man's name was Noel.

I went off to sleep, to be woken by the kettle being put on the stove and another big pot with about 30 boiled eggs in it – breakfast. Noel came down from where he had been sleeping for the night and said he had to try and get a drink somewhere. We emptied our pockets – a few coins and a packet of Rizzla cigarette paper and nothing else.

There was a hay barn at the back of the Simon and when the hostel was full some of the men would sleep there. It was a foggy morning and Noel said 'I know where I can get a good drink'. It was

Sunday morning and the pubs didn't open till later so I had no idea of where he was going. He just told me to wait where I was. As he disappeared into the fog I didn't expect to see him again.

Then after about half an hour I heard this clanging noise coming through the fog. It was Noel and he was rolling something. As he got closer I could see he had got a barrel of Harp Larger off the Dublin to Belfast train, where it stops for five minutes before heading on for Newry.

He was my hero! All the men came out of the Simon with their tea mugs. Noel got a hammer and opened the barrel. We sat on a hay bail and drunk mugs of larger. The word got out and more road men - mostly alcoholics who travelled the roads of the country and who were fthe inspiration for Sr Consilio's work - arrived to have a drink.

Noel and I hung around together. He was such as funny bloke. On Monday we headed for the dole office. I signed on at 2.00 but Noel signed on before then, at 9.30. So he bought me a good drink and I returned the favour in the afternoon.

He asked me later did I want him to look after my money and keep it safe in his sock. I, for whatever reason, did just that. I trusted him and it wasn't a mistake. He gave the money back to me

Tuesday morning. I told him to keep looking after it, as I might lose it and we headed for the nearby convent where the nuns were to get a feed. Me and Noel didn't spend drinking money on food when, as he said to me, there is a perfectly good convent up the road, with free food.

The nuns in these convents were mostly very sound women. I mean, how many doors can you knock on and get invited in for a meal, especially if the people know you are on the drink. But that was what they did. They often came in while we were eating and sat down at the table and chatted with us. Some would open up to us and talk about their own life and how they came to join the nuns.

Some of the older nuns might say that marriage wasn't an option for them – but that they had kind of grown into a life that they found well worthwhile. There were other women who had lots of options and, you could see, joined out of real conviction. Sr Consilio could have married and had a family, had a career in nursing or teaching or working at anything really. But she said to me one time that she knew it was God's plan for her and that in following this plan she ended up with her own very special family and in making a home for all kinds of people in trouble of one kind or another.

My husband and life-long best friend Noel

Noel and I were often glad to have a convent
to call on to get a meal! It was always a bit of an

adventure in calling at the convent or the priest's house. I remember one time Noel said to me 'There's a priest down the road who is due a visit to get a few pounds – we'll go in separately'. So I hid around the corner; in went Noel and got a fiver. I went in after him and the priest told me that a man was in just before me who was also in need of help and he had no change left. I said 'That's okay, I'll take a note'. He told me to 'Go on, now'. He was in a hurry but he still gave me £2.50. Off with me and Noel to the off-licence to get some 'liquid refreshment', as Noel called it.

The breathalyser catches up with us

Three times Noel got done for the breathalyser while driving – in Dundalk, in Drogheda and in Dublin. The police caught up with Noel and me in Newry, which is just over the border in Northern Ireland. An empty bus had been set on fire – that was when there were big troubles in Northern Ireland. As we came up Daisy Hill, the police pulled us over. They men had actually let us go, but a police woman stuck her nose in the window and said she could smell drink.

So they breathalysed Noel and he was taken to the police station. They left him with a full bottle of vodka – which we had put into an orange bottle! Because of this, they didn't recognise what it was or they would certainly have confiscated it. They left our car, a Ford Escort, on the High Street. This was about 7.30 in the evening.

They released Noel at about 12pm and when I came back to the car, there he was waiting for me with the vodka in the orange bottle; he hadn't drunk all of it. Noel took a few slugs of the vodka and we decided to head down to his family in Kildare, who I hadn't met. On the way down, we picked up a man, somewhere between Dundalk and Drogheda, which is on the south side of the Irish border. Our passenger was also an alcoholic and we shared a small drop of our drink with him, as we were running low and running out of luck.

It was the Gardaí – the Irish police - who pulled us over this time. They were looking for the same fella that we had picked up. They then put the breathalyser on Noel. This was about 2am and off with Noel again to the Garda station. They released him after about an hour and a half without charge. They gave Noel the car and keys and told him to be careful on the rest of our travels. But they arrested the passenger. We never found out what happened to him.

We then drove out of town for about three or four miles and parked our car and finished whatever drink we had. Bad luck was still with us. About 7am that morning as we were passing through Finglas – which is in Dublin – the Gardaí again pulled us over. They breathalysed Noel and then said they couldn't release him unless he could produce bail money. Noel had no cash on him. He did have a bank book with £500. This was money he had left in the bank, from years before. It was Saturday morning and the bank wasn't opened so he gave the police a cheque.

This meant we had to wait until Monday morning for the bank to open. Noel got £100 from his brother John. This helped us out, with plenty of liquid refreshments while we stayed at John's house. Our big concern was whether we could beat the Gardaí to the bank on the Monday morning. Noel no longer had his Bank book – having had to leave it with the Gardaí. But Noel's brothers were well known in the bank in Athy and we knew they would remember Noel.

We waited from 9.30 until the bank opened at 10.00. We were first into the bank and Noel knew one of the cashiers and went to him and told him he lost his bank book. So he gave Noel the £500. He left 15p to keep the account open and we decided it must be time to celebrate. We stayed out all that day and arrived at John's house sometime in the early morning. But old habits die hard and we headed for the hay shed out the back with a couple of bottles.

An Abtract Painting

Finding 'Mugs'

There are so many things that can happen, often when you don't expect them. When Noel and I were living in our house in Parkhead Crescent, Newry, we would sign on in Dundalk and then stay overnight in the Simon. I met an old road man – these were the men forced to move around the country that, as I said earlier, Sr. Consilio started-out by helping. He was called 'Charlie Scouse'.

We told him we had a fine house in Newry and he was welcome to stay with us. I remember this was on a Thursday. By Sunday morning the money was almost gone. The two of us decided we would try and get hold of some money for drink.

It wasn't always easy to get drink in Newry. But there was this one pub on the Point road where you could tap on the window – Molly's was the name of it and you would get a drink out at the 'back door'. So we managed to get a drink there and after we got the drink down us we decided we would try the Salvation Army and see if they would they give us a few pounds.

We had been everywhere else in the past few weeks. Now we were going to the Salvation Army – God bless them. Noel said 'Okay, today I am going

76

to be deaf and dumb!' I started talking to the two Salvation Army women and explained how we were poverty stricken and my husband was deaf and dumb. The lady said it was very unfortunate – and then she tried to communicate with Noel in sign language. Noel didn't know any sign language. Then she said she wasn't very good at sign language herself and 'it was a pity that you weren't here yesterday because one of the ladies was fluent in sign language'!

She asked for my address which I gave her and she said she would meet us at our house in about half an hour to an hour. We had a good mile to walk home but we hadn't told her that 'Charlie Scouse' was there. When we remembered, we made a mad rush to get there be by three o'clock, before they got there.

As we arrived at our house, up a steep hill, we saw that they were waiting there with three bags of shopping. I then had to rush in tell Charlie Scouse: 'Listen, pretend you are Noel's uncle and you've just arrived from Liverpool – and remember, Noel is deaf and dumb'.

I nearly pissed myself laughing when Charlie Scouse put his two arms around Noel and gave him a kiss and said 'Noel, I haven't seen you for years'. Turning to me Charlie said 'I hope you didn't mind me letting myself in but I looked under the mat and found the key'. Charlie was very quick – he was in front of the two women; otherwise they would wonder how he got into the house.

But this was the least of our problems. We had been to the Convent during the week and done well. Noel had been working for a few days. So, our fridge was well stocked-up. Food was the furthest thing from our mind. It was money for drink we wanted. But they arrived with three bags of shopping – enough to feed us for a fortnight! I grabbed the bags and took them into the room where I said we had a freezer because the fridge couldn't be opened! The two ladies sat down and it looked to me were in for a long drawn out conversation.

This was when Noel started to make what sounded like a few grunting noises; he had never before spent longer than five or ten seconds without saying something – anything. This grunting was repeated on a number of occasions. The good woman from the Salvation Army was still trying to communicate with Noel by sign language.

But we weren't having any success with getting any money – and Noel was getting more frustrated with every 'grunt'. I then suggested to the two Salvation Army women that maybe Charlie was tired and needed a bit of rest. Charlie said that seems like a good idea, as he was travelling all night.

I was glad and mighty relieved when they were finally gone. We thought things could only improve so we took the food stuff they had brought back to the shop where they bought it. But the shop wouldn't take back the food, so the three of us set back into town to where the Travellers where staying on the 'line' – which was a long stretch of waste land by the river. We traded off the shopping for a bottle of QC wine, three bottles of cider and ten fags. After we got the drink down us and did a bit of begging here and there - it turned out a pretty good evening. But I would have to say that it was the hardest days' work I've ever done!

Sleeping In the Skip

While we were living in our house in Newry, Noel and I would have the odd argument or two. We had one argument that went on for about three or four days. Between drinking and arguing we sometimes went our separate ways, out the door to go drinking.

But one day something happened. I don't know if I had a blackout.. The thing was – I wound up in Belfast. I still had some money in my sock. So between shaking with the drink and being frozen with cold and not having a clue where I was, I headed for the off licence.

This was the first time I had spotted 'Mundays' wine. The bottles didn't look as big as the old 'QC' wine. I used to get two of them. One I paid for but, being a bit of a pig for drink that I was in those days – and, as the day had gone past on me and I didn't know where I'd been – I drank one of the bottles fairly quickly.

On that particular occasion, and with Noel back in the house in Newry, I still don't know if I ever drank the second bottle because I remember nothing more of that night. Until the next morning: when a man – an early morning worker – woke me up. I was covered in snow and I had been sleeping in a skip!

He said 'You had better get out of there, and quickly, because there will be a skip wagon along shortly'. I was shaking with the cold. He took his coat off and threw it over me. I am pretty sure that he must have been an alcoholic himself and he gave me a £5 note and told me a shop nearby would be open soon were I could get a 'cure'.

I went to the shop where I see the Mundays wine the day before. This time I only got one bottle because there wasn't a 'two for one' offer on this occasion. I drank the wine a little more carefully this time and began heading back to Noel. When I got back to Newry I headed for our usual place by the canal. There was Noel plus a few travellers and plenty of drink. We made up later that day and headed for home. Noel suggested we go and have a drink in the pub. But none of the pubs would serve me – they would serve Noel but I was barred. I was a bit of a Jekyll and Hyde character when I was in the drink.

Noel found this happening in nearly every town we went to. So, we would have to drink on the park bench instead. Pubs were out for me and often I was too well known to go into an off licence. They would know I would put a bottle under my coat. But

Noel sometimes would distract them, keeping them talking until I got out the shop. Then I would hand the bottle to Noel and they would chase him, instead of me. No one could catch Noel – he was a very fast runner. He needed to be.

He would come back when the coast was clear. We would drink that bottle and then do the same again. Or next time he might fake an epileptic fit as he entered a new off licence. They would come from behind the counter to help him while another of them would go out back to phone an ambulance. I would stash a bottle of brandy for Noel and a bottle of vodka for me into the pockets of my long black coat – they were like Fagan's pockets, on the inside of the coat.

I had never trusted anyone since Monica, the artist who befriended me back in the day. But Noel was different and I knew I could trust him completely. My bond with Noel made life a lot easier for me: he got me out of a lot of scrapes and we were always laughing.

Usually we could get money one way or another. Noel could always get a few days' work, as he was so good at contracting work. But when he was drinking heavy he wouldn't be able to work. Then Noel would stand on one side of the street with me on the other, telling stories of misfortune of one kind or another in order for the people passing by to part with some cash. Sometimes I had so many 50p and £1 pieces that when I ran you could hear the loose change rattle. I would have to hold on to the pocket as I ran after someone who I had missed and looked a likely candidate. The craic was mighty.

Noel and I got a house in Derry Bay and we were happy there for a while, signing on in Newry as well as in Dundalk. But one time Noel got caught 'doing the double'. The men approached him and said 'Noel, it's no good denying it, this is your signature.' 'Okay' Noel said to them, 'I'll pay you back, when I get paid in up the road in about 15 minutes'. They looked at him in horror: 'you certainly will not be receiving any moneys from this office or from Newry' they said. So, Noel said 'You know my address. Write to me'. Now was time to move.

'Shopping Trips'

When we were drinking 'moderately' Noel would manage to get work at least three or four days at a time, by tarmacking and rubbish clearance. On one occasion, Noel gave me £10 to go shopping. He liked steak and he liked a drop of brandy, when he had the money. But that was the only £10 he had to give me for the next 2 weeks. Noel asked me every night if I wanted money for shopping and I said, 'No' – that I still have the £10. The thing was, I had this new coat I had stolen out of Oxfam which had 'magnetic pockets'.

While Noel sat down and tucked into his usual steak and half bottle of brandy, I sat down with my half bottle of vodka watching telly. As usual when the drink was finished we would then head off for the off licence, where we would 'buy one and get one free'! This was just one of many of our shopping expeditions, including trips to the off licence.

Noel would sometimes say that his old rags were getting bad from work. So I would extend my shopping trip to the second-hand shops and sometimes the new shops. When Noel would come home in the evening he might have a choice of a suit or trousers and a jacket. Sometimes the trousers might be too long, or the sleeves might be too long as he has short arms and legs. But with a few drinks down us I would tell Noel 'we can exchange these tomorrow for something better'.

Sometimes the clothes might not fit Noel. So I used to wear his trousers into the shop and then I would try a new pair out and hang the old pair back on the hanger and put them on the rack. When the shop keeper asked me if I'd found anything I liked, I would say there was something but I need to go home and loose a few pounds and I would thank her very much and leave the shop. I would then head down the canal where Noel would be waiting, with our usual supply of drink.

Thinking about Marriage

Sometimes when Noel got wages for work he would put money on a horse. One day he put money on Desert Orchid and it won. He got £1,400! He asked me 'Okay, Anne do you want to go on holiday?' I said I would enjoy a holiday better with a drink, so he said 'Okay, we will go to the off licence instead'. It was only the beginning of January and that particular binge lasted till March. We had to go to hospital to dry out again. But before we ran out of money I had to go to the chemist to get some meth (methylated spirit). We would mix it with water, so it looked to anyone watching us like we were drinking milk as it turned white. It would stop the shakes.

Another time I couldn't get served meth's so I took some 'Old Spice' aftershave and drunk it. I must have had sweet smelling breath for an alcoholic and it made me feel better because it alcohol in it. When I look back, I really abused myself in order to stop the terrible shaking in my head, hands and that feeling you are going to pass out.

I was laughing with Noel one day by the canal and he said I was a lot of fun to be with – quite mental! So I said lets gets married. 'Okay, so' said Noel, 'we will ask the Priest in a minute when we go for money to marry us'. It would have been around

1985. We went to the priest and after he gave us a bit of change Noel said 'Oh Father, we are getting married, will you marry us?'; 'What's your address?' he asked Noel and then he asked me the same question. 'Oh no', he said 'you are living in sin you will go to hell'! Noel said there isn't enough room for everyone that includes you. So, we got married in a registry office and Noel's family came to have a look at his wife.

We spent the next day and then the next two weeks celebrating, slowly making our way back to Newry, and stopping at every convent and priests house on the way. When we got back to Newry we were given a voucher for £600 from St. Vincent De Paul for a new bed, clothes and other bits of furniture, which of course we didn't buy. We were also due to sign on the dole the following day. But that turned out to be when we got caught for signing on the dole twice.

Two days after Noel was caught we decided to go to Newry as common law husband and wife. We didn't have anywhere to stay when we arrived as Noel had been living on the Line; this was beside the Canal in Newry with the Travellers. As we got into Newry Noel said 'we'll get ourselves a squat'. So we did. There was an empty house opposite the dole office and we stayed there for about a month until…

Well, we were signing on the dole as common law man and wife. We had been paid on the Friday, and, as usual, we had extra drink taken and slept late. Then we heard some banging. Eventually we went to investigate (after getting a 'cure' down us).

There was a man, from the Council I suppose, actually boarding up the house that we were squatting in. All the windows were blocked up and he almost had the door blocked up, too. When we appeared downstairs trying to get out, he unblocked the door. He was a nice fellow and he got the original door and put it back on, so we could at least get another week there. Down by the canal was like a home for us; we often slept there at night and we would eat pilchards and dry bread. There were also two Convents, three Priests and four or five different churches within walking distance and which we visited daily.

Good days in Parkhead Crescent

While we were on the bank of the canal a couple of social workers would come by see how we were getting on. They said they would put us forward for a place to live. They would ask us a lot of questions and we would give them all the answers they wanted to hear, just to get rid of them and if they weren't leaving quick enough we would ask them for money. Like most people, they wouldn't stay long when you asked for money.

But there was one of the social workers that wouldn't go so quickly; still we never thought anything would come of her visits. One day she came and asked us to come with her to her office. Luckily we didn't have that much to drink that day, so we went along with her. Surprise! They offered us a choice of two houses, one in Parkhead Crescent and one Cambala in Derry Beg. We went in her car to look at Parkhead Crescent. It looked like a palace compared to what we were used to. We agreed to take it and they said we could move in within the week. With the help of the St Vincent De Paul we soon had a bed, table, and a two seater settee.

At this stage we were getting pretty rough from drink, squatting and sleeping rough. We attended the doctors at least three times a week trying to get valium. On the last day we attended, the doctor must have thought we needed some additional help. He said that we should go into hospital to try and get off the drink and recommended St Luke's in Armagh. We agreed to go so they got an ambulance to take us there that day. We must have been very shattered although neither of us could see this at the time.

There was a shop in Newry that, if you were living in a house, would let you rent a colour TV; we got one for £1.50 a week for the first two weeks. This was a complete novelty for us. We would watch coloured television, have plenty of drinks and were able to have a pot of stew on the stove. But all this soon went by the wayside; the drink itself seemed a far better novelty. We were there about six months in that house but we still used to visit the canal every day.

All about getting married

It was there we decided to get married. Then things happened, the way they sometimes do. On our way home that evening I tripped over a pavement stone and fell into the bushes. As we had a lot of drink taken, as usual, we took no notice of it at the time but the next morning I was sore and I had a cut on my head.

Noel took me to the hospital. We had talked to each other about giving up the drink and trying to get sober for our wedding. When we were at the hospital the doctor said 'you are not the first person to have an accident over the paving stones' and suggested we should see a lawyer. After coming out of the hospital we still had a drink with us. After a few drinks, and when you don't have a lot of money, it didn't take much to get us to go to the solicitor's office.

When we were in St Luke's hospital some social workers came to visit us and started to give us advice on getting a place of our own and how to go about it. But the truth of the matter was we were saving a few valium and planning the next session of drink. As all alcoholics know, when you're in detox for more than two weeks, it is not exactly how you visualise your life, especially in our particular case. Noel and I had no family, no home but we did have

91

plenty of good advice which, in fairness, we later put to good use.

So, we got up one morning in St Luke's, as we were free to go in and out, and we decided to go out and stay out! Our first stop was Newry where Noel had met all the Travellers and it didn't take much coaxing when we were invited to John Wards son's wedding.

Emily and Paddy

Back to Square one – in and out of the Canal

We went to the wedding and started to drink. We were back at square one. This continued for the next four weeks. We used to sit by the canal, bottles of cider, wine mixed with mentholated spirit and any alcohol we could get. This was known as 'Dr Noel's special'. One time around then we were sitting by the canal and we had an argument. I went to grab the bottle from Noel and he pushed me away from the bottle. I rolled down the slope and straight into the canal. I still had the can of pilchards I had lifted that morning.

Noel tried to lean down and pull me out but he couldn't reach me. So he jumped down and then lifted me up. It took about twenty minutes, as it was slimy and slippery because the tide was out. Noel was trying and trying to lift me up and push me onto the bank, when a man, passing by, shouted asking Noel if he wanted some help. 'Yeah' Noel said 'I do'.

They got me out but it was so slippery that Noel himself couldn't get out. So, a few more people came along; one of them took off their coat, Noel held onto it and they pulled him up from the canal. A normal person would have gone home for a bath and change of clothes but since we didn't have a bath or a change of clothes, we just said the sun will dry them.

Afterwards, we went back by the canal, had another few drinks and we started to discuss our wedding date. The solicitor had told us that morning that it would take about six months to get the claim through. We'd have the money to get married on the 7th of the month and it couldn't have worked out any better – we got the money about the end of sixth month. We had our date set for the wedding on the 16th.

Our claim was granted about the first week of September and the solicitor called us into his office. We had been drinking for quite a while at this stage so, having the cheek of the devil, we decided to ask the solicitor for an advance and he gave us £250 out of the £1000 we had been granted.

We now could take a rest from begging for a few days and instead of picking up 'dog ends' we could now buy fags. The £250 didn't last very long. On the Monday morning after that we had spent the last of the dole money. We were outside the solicitor's office again and he gave us another £250 – that kept us going for a few days.

During this time there was no talk of the wedding. The following Monday morning was a repeat of the previous one, and the same the following week. We went to see the solicitor and we asked for another advance and he said 'I can give it all to you today' not realising that we only had £250 left and we still had a few days to go before our wedding.

He gave us the final £250 owed to us and we went off to buy a wedding ring but we were still under the influence and decided that £12 was enough to pay for a wedding ring. We then decided to extend our celebrations and these continued until the morning of our wedding. When we woke up, slightly late, we were penniless. We did have one bottle of vodka which we were well into before we realised we were due to get married that same morning.

I went up to get dressed. I had stolen a suit from the second hand shop but the skirt belonged to one suite and the jacket to another. Noels family were to come for the wedding and Clare Cody was to be my bridesmaid. But because we were drunk we had forgotten that Clare had arranged to meet us at the reception area of the Registry office.

Noel's family were late arriving so I went across to the train station to see if they had come by train. I met all these young people who asked me who I was waiting for and I told them I was waiting for Noel's family and my bridesmaid, as I was getting married. So one little girl said 'I'll be your bridesmaid' and I said 'Okay' and at least six of them came back to the house. After about half an hour Noel's family arrived in a minibus.

On the wedding day itself, we had spent all our money on drink so Noel's brother, John, who had hired a minibus to come to the wedding, had to pay. The woman thought because he paid, he was the one marrying me. I can tell you, the Registry Office was no Church; it was more like a court house.

We went off to the pub with all the Bradleys (Noel's family), about 20 of them, and had a great day. But when we went back to the pub to the reception, we were barred. Someone had nicked the chain of the gas bottles the day of the wedding – it was one of Noel's cousins. He had taken the chain to tie to the gate to keep the cows in at home.

Scotland: Fire!....Shoes!....and hot toddy's!

After a few drinks, and with a couple of breathalyser charges on Noel's head, it was time to leave and go further afield. We had to leave Newry. We also had no intention of paying back the dole money so we headed for London. Noel's friend Harry Nolan would give work on the buildings straight away. Noel was always very bright. He could design a block of flats and also carry out all manual work underpinning… anything.

So when we got to London Noel started work the next day. He left me a few pounds and told me to stay at Harry's house and not touch the booze! I walked into the front room and there round the skirting boards were hundreds of miniatures – whisky, vodka, brandy, gin. So I got a pint glass and put a tiny bit into this glass. When the boys came back I was well out of it. That was it. Noel told me 'we can't stay now, you blew it'. So we set course for Scotland. I'd put my thumb up to hitch a lift and when a car stopped Noel would jump in, to their surprise. Off we went with the second hand suitcases, with a change of clothes from the second-hand shop. We got to the main motorway and then stayed together as the lorries would pick you up, no problem – you being there would help keep them awake when they were driving long distances. We only stopped once for a drink before the off-licence closed and then headed for Glasgow. A car beeping his horn drove alongside us, with a suitcase hanging out the window. The lorry driver said 'it's not mine'; Noel shouted 'it's mine'. We stopped at the next lay by and retrieved the suitcase from the Good Samaritan. It had fallen off the back of the truck. The lorry driver was laughing his head off and on we went again. He liked us so much he dropped us right in the Gorbles, at the heart of Glasgow.

We headed for the hostel that the driver had told us about. But they could only take Noel so we searched for some sort of shelter for the night. We found a kind of shelter but couldn't tell what it was, because it was pitch black. Noel lit a fire and I went for some more sticks and got some old logs.

When I got back I could see this bright red 'glow'. But there was no sign of Noel – just billowing smoke. But what he had were some crocodile shoes which I had got from the second hand shop that morning and it was these that I spotted them. So I pulled at his feet and that was how I pulled him out of the smoke.

Out he came too, and I was laughing so much: he was as black as a pot. 'Where's the drink?' he asked. 'In there in the fire', I said. I had a duffle coat that I got that day in the same place as his shoes.

So he put this coat over his head and back with him into the smoke to retrieve the drink. He was only gone for a few minutes but by this time the flames were lapping at the ceiling of what had turned out to be an old warehouse with wardrobes and tables and loads of cardboard. I could hear the fire brigade coming when Noel ran through the smoke to where I was standing, about 200 metres from the fire. He had the cans wrapped up in the duffle coat and the whisky in his pocket. 'Here', he said 'had a hot toddy'.

I couldn't help laughing again, he wasn't just black as a pot - but his eyebrows were gone as well, and his hair was singed. But still, it was 'mission accomplished' when he put the cans in the snow to cool down. Then he said 'when we drink these few cans, we'll head off now - we can always sleep later'. So, we headed back to London where Noel had the address of an old mate Gerry Ryley, over by Wandsworth Common.

We arrived early in the morning. Gerry was already tucking into a lagoon of cider or two. He introduced us to the Landlord, Reg, who was a real character. He said that Noel and I could rent a room – a large room – in Henderson Road. Gerry gave Noel a loan – no problem, as everyone knew that Noel always paid back. Gerry was from Connemara and had met Noel in the 60's. He was hilarious.

There was another alcoholic there called 'Top'. He was someone who also worked, and drank, hard - as we were to find out. We gave Reg the £30 rent for the week, in advance. He sent us up to the off licence to bring home as much drink as we could buy for the money which Noel had just given him!

What a house! We stayed there a while but put our name down on the Council list straight away for a flat. After about 6 months paying rent to Reg, and going to the off licence, we got a flat in Battersea. It was a grand place, just opposite Battersea Park – where the houses were worth millions.

Back to London...

By 1990 or so, we moved from Scotland to London to a place called Norwood. Noel was on the dole. At that time, after being a short time on the dole they would send you to the Job Centre to get a job. So we arrived at the Job Centre (we had had a fair few drinks down us) where they would be interviewing Noel for a job.

Noel worked on the buildings for years and had loads of experience. But on this one occasion neither Noel nor I wanted any type of work, as work would interfere with our life. So at the start of the interview the man said 'Noel, what type of work would you like?' Noel thought for a minute and said in a funny voice – 'something with a bit of responsibility'. I had to make a dash for the toilet and get myself together, from laughing.

I came back a few minutes later; the man had left his chair and had gone to get some leaflets which he passed to Noel. But Noel said 'I can't read or write'. I explained to the man that I would read the leaflets to him later on. Noel then said again 'I just want something with a small bit of responsibility'. During the interview he kept tapping his head. The man asked me if there was something wrong with Noel. I said he had been fine, until the brick fell on his head. I turned to ask Noel if everything was alright. He said 'Anne, will I tell them that I used to be an alcoholic?' I told him he had better tell the man everything. Noel took half bottle of vodka from his inside pocket and said to the man, 'I used to drink three or four of these during the day, if I could get them – or any other kind of alcohol or methylated spirit'.

Then I said, as if to reassure the man, that he was only drinking a half bottle a day. Noel started tapping his head again – it was time for him to go to the toilet and get a slug of drink.

I went back to see the man before Noel came out of the toilet and I asked him how did the interview go. He said 'I think he's (Noel!) over the hill. If you hold on a minute I'll give you a letter to give to his doctor'. We then left the job centre and resumed our place on the park bench!

Finding my Birth Mother...That was a long time ago!

I really wanted to track down my natural parents, my birth mother. I have to say that this was just some instinct inside me. It wasn't that I wanted someone different from that wonderful woman who had been 'mother' to me through all of my ups and downs. It was just something inside of me that wanted to know and to help me understand 'Anne' and, perhaps, why she had put me up for adoption. That's why I wanted to track her down.

We had been waiting quite a few months to hear from the Adoption Society. In those days, it used to be the case that with the files closed and not available to be looked at – this was going back in my case to 1955 – you couldn't track down your birth parents. But we heard that they could do research and we thought 'well, maybe they could research this information on my natural mum for me'. Noel helped me organize the search and paid for it.

One day the information arrived in a letter. 'Marjorie' was my birth mothers name and she had an address in Dagenham. I was curious to meet her but the main thing was that I had actually found her. Noel and I arrived at the house.

I couldn't believe it at first, but had to laugh afterwards when I thought back on how I was feeling as I walked up to her door. There was no answer at first and then a voice shouted 'the keys in the door'.

I had the strangest reaction at our first meeting. We walked in and she was sitting in an armchair with a shawl around her. We said 'Hello, Marjorie'. I had a big file with me on my lap. I told her I was born in June 1955 and had every reason to believe I was her daughter. She looked at me for about a minute and then said '1955; well, that's a long time ago. I can't remember that far back'. I thought: 'for f…sake, you had your child put up for adoption – you must remember that'.

It was as if we were discussing an unpaid electric bill. After a bit Noel asked her did she have a child to a Frankie Joslin – that was the name of the natural father on the information we had got – and she said she did. Noel said 'well, he is Anne's father, so you must be Anne's birth mother'. 'Very well', she said 'pleased to meet you!' And she shook my hand.

She didn't have much talk so we asked her a few questions. She had photos of a lad of about twenty in an army uniform, with a girl beside him. I asked her who they were and she replied 'that's my son Peter; he is very good to me'. Big news!

So I had a brother and the girl was his wife, Rosanna. I gave her a photo of me as a baby; she put it on her table quickly and asked us to make tea. Noel went for a while so as to leave me and Marjorie to talk. I was with her for about 15 minutes and I asked her about my father. His name, like I said, was Frankie. She asked me, 'where is he now? I haven't seen him for years'. I knew she didn't want to talk about it but I felt she owed me something so I gently asked her what he was like. She looked up and said 'he looked a bit like you – tall and handsome and he was the love of my life'.

We spoke some more and she said to me out of the blue, 'I thought you were the nurse coming to bathe my legs when you knocked the door, that's why the door was open'. So I got a bowl of warm water and she reluctantly took off her slippers and put her feet in the bowl, 'Thank you - what's your name again? Anne, oh yes, Anne'.

I spoke about my adoptive mum and dad and how they were very special and had treated me as their own child in every way. I told her I had been searching for her a long time and I was glad I'd found her. She said the days at the government-run 'Mother and baby Home' were bad; some of the mothers, she said, never were the same again, crying for weeks when their babies were snatched from their arms and taken away.

106

Then she told me 'Your Dad was from Dublin'. A lot of things suddenly made sense. I asked if she had a photo of him. She didn't; 'No, I only have a photo of Peter'. Noel came back and we got ready to leave. I got Peter's address after she had rooted in a box for a while and told her I would return very soon and she said 'goodbye'.

We had a phone number for Peter and his wife, Rosanna. I was keen to find Peter. So I picked up the phone and called them. We had a chat and arranged to meet at Kew Gardens. I liked him straight away and we had the same sense of humour.

Years later after our children were born Peter, Rosanna and their two girls headed off to Disneyland Paris, and our Sean and Paddy came as well. We've never had a babysitter, only once when Paddy was born and that was Noel's sister, Emily. When we came back from France we were friends. The following summer Peter's family came to Kildare and met his 'other family' in Ireland. But we couldn't find my father, Frankie Joslin from Dublin, and we are still looking.

Peter, Joanne, Sophie, Sean, Judy and Me

We often went to stay at Auntie Emilys house in Derby and we would head for the Nugents, Liz, Jimmy, Billy, Henry, Sean and Paddy like playing football as Billy had a great touch and was quality at football.

Liz & Billy

Billy was playing for Derby County at the time.

Henry, Liz's youngest son went on to join the Royal Marines.

Liz and me get on really well, she has a great attitude to life, she's such a laugh and a great person to talk too when things become out of focus. Over the years she has always told me to write a book or a get job helping alcoholics or something that I would love doing.

Henry & Paddy at Roger Ingram's yard

From Addiction to Sobriety

I know – none better – how difficult it is to stop drinking for more than a few days at a time. There has to be something there, something real that is more important to you than the drink. Looking at it today, I really had nothing to look forward, to even after me and Noel had got married. We still never had anything to take us beyond ourselves; it was just one thing, and one place, after another and always the drink there inside our heads.

Then we thought of trying to have a family. We went to different clinics but they couldn't find any reason why I couldn't get pregnant. So we carried on as usual, on, and off, the drink for the next couple of years. But having a family of our own was something that was always there – always important

Then one day we went back once again to the hospital to find out if they could tell us anything more at all about why it was I still couldn't get pregnant. In the hospital they recommended we go to the clinic in Brook Green, London where they did some tests. At that particular time we had been off the drink about two weeks. They told us to come back in two weeks for the results. When we returned they told us that for as long as we continued to drink like we were, I would never get pregnant. We left the

112

hospital feeling very contented with ourselves because what that meant was that if we did stop drinking – and kept off it – then we might be able to have children after all. But being two alcoholics together we had to celebrate the good news that if we changed and cut out the drink it might be that we could have kids.

This 'celebration' led to what was probably one of the longest binges of all, starting just before Christmas and not ending until the second week in April. It was in the middle of this session that we kept talking about having kids. On the second week Brendan, a friend of Noel's, called to the house for him to come and do some work. We had made a decision the day before. I think we had both taken alcoholic seizures when we were withdrawing from the drink.

Noel went to work with his friend Brendan and I stayed in bed, as I was very ill. It was only a few hours before Brendan returned with Noel. Brendan told me Noel had taken a seizure in the café. Brendan then gave us some money to go to the off licence to get Noel a drink; I got two litres of Cider and a bottle of Vodka. We both drank the vodka and some of the cider; I know we didn't drink all of it.

We knew that we wouldn't be able to have kids if we didn't decide to go off the drink. We had to try. I said we will go off the drink for four months; Noel said six – as 'if we didn't really try we'd never know, okay? I said if I don't get pregnant, can I go back on the drink then? 'okay' said Noel.

Noel went back to work after a few days' rest; and was on his bike every day. About three months later I went ot the doctor to be told I was pregnant! , so I surprised Noel at the door when he came home from work! That was so real. Noel just said 'Do you realise babies are expensive, more expensive than drink!' We then decided it was time to focus on buying our own house for our own family. Whatever about the four or six months, we never went back on the drink.

Paddy - Start of his career

Pride and Joy: our two Boys

Sean was born on 23rd July, a day after
Granny's Birthday. My Mum and Dad were so
happy. I had now a chance to also make amends to
my parents by staying sober. Sean was gorgeous, fit
and well. Noel worked hard, as babies cost money.
He was so proud. Just when I thought God had given
me a miracle I received another one – I was pregnant
again. Paddy was born with red hair and blue eyes –
he was gorgeous.

115

Noel had formed 'CAE Building Services' and had bought me a Nissan Terrano just to take the kids to school as before Sean was born I went on my last driving test – I was 8 ½ months pregnant and I passed! We went out for a feed at Wimpy to celebrate my victory after failing three times. Noel had taken the afternoon off.

When they were very little, I'd often look at Sean and Paddy in bed, as they never slept in a cot. We had two double beds put together for them; it was so cosy. They would get put in there when I was cleaning and managing the house.

After the children were a bit older, I told Noel my nose wasn't right because of all the battering I'd got. He said when I get the cheque you can have a nose job. Noel paid about £6,000 for two nose jobs, as the first one didn't look right still. Noel's very good with money but if the children need anything they would always get it even if he had to do without himself. And the same if I need something, he will always make sure we get it.

This is what I had given up the drink for and it was the best thing I had ever done. I know that staying sober is a challenge for some people: I understand that. There has to be something that helps you make that transition from drinking to a different kind of life – something that lasts. I knew I had been given a chance to be a good mum, and when they got bigger, they would treat me as a mate. As they got older they would wind me up – and their humour had no mercy; and it still doesn't.

Paddy and Sean hated school. So, after a few writs about me going to court for not getting them into school at all, I gave up. It didn't seem right they weren't happy. I understood, wasn't I the same? Two friends Mark and Hayley – two amazing Christian people Sean had met from working at the Youth Centre in Waters Edge called to the house to help me tell the authorities that I would 'home tutor' Paddy; Sean wasn't doing much anyway. I wouldn't mind, but Paddy was ten times cleverer than me. If he had done any work – which he didn't – he could have been teaching me, not the other way round. In the end, I took Sean out of school as well. School wasn't for them. They had different talents and I knew they would do really well.

Coming home to Mum and Dad.

From the time Sean and Paddy were born my Mum and Dad once again became a big part of my own life – and their dreams; Paddy wanting to be a Jockey and Sean a footballer. It is amazing how things just came round again – and this time it was so positive, as if everything in my own early life had been made whole again – as it had really.

My mum and Dad adored the children and the children loved them so much. I often hugged my Dad and Mum and they would squeeze me back. My Dad would say 'Don't be sorry for all that happened, we knew you would come back okay someday'. Mum said she was certain of that, as she prayed for me all the time and never gave up on me – ever.

I had eleven years sobriety that I could share with them before they died – Mum first and then Dad. R.I.P. I came back to them and visited every summer; they were as close to two angels I have ever met. I was so blessed to have them as my parents. I know that now. Christine became a very successful teacher, had four children and has been happily married. She doesn't keep in contact – just a card at Christmas. It is sad really that we couldn't have become friends. But I am glad she is happy.

Football, and only football, with Sean

Sean was always good at sport and especially football. He joined a team called Wandle Wanderers. Gus was the manager with his wife Yvonne. Their kids were Ike, Obi and Kerry. Obi who was very good at football was Paddy's friend and Paddy joined the team. Iki was Sean's friend. Whenever they changed to a better team Sean would change to be with Iki and Iki would do the same; they are good mates and have been since they were six years old.

Boys from Brazil to join Chelsea- Noel and Gus, Football agents also iki and obie

Sean joined Woking Football Academy when he was just fifteen until he reached eighteen. Before that he was with Charlton, but they released him due to injury.

Sean is gifted at playing football. Always has been. Noel and Gus, who was a football manager, went into business promoting players from Brazil, Nigeria, Portugal and here in England. Noel got involved so that he would be in a position to help get Sean into good clubs later on. He is brilliant at coaching and I believe that is where his talents will really show through.

Sean has been going for his coaching badges since fifteen and soon after his sixteenth birthday received his level 1 badge. He has modules as well, so he is building up for his UEFA B Badge. He has coached Level Three with the Swedish 1st Team girls in Sweden and has been offered work the second time he was there. He is going for Trials in Sweden with the 1st Team in 2014. Sean is living his dream and Noel's Company CAE always sponsored Sean's team.

Sean, footballer and coach.

For Noel and me to know Sean is working

with really good teams is incredible – he is playing
semi-pro. One day he will be working at an even
higher level. As a coach or a pro footballer, with his
(UEFA B) he has to get £900 to go for this but that
day is not far away. He has already achieved a whole
lot, especially to have become such a highly qualified
coach at 22. He has so much skill with a ball, it
would take your breath away. Like Paddy he was
given a very special gift and I am blessed to have had
them including Noel who can turn his hand to any
kind of building work.

Going Racing with Paddy

Paddy was good at football too. But his heart was always in horse racing, he wanted to be a jockey. From the time he was five years old he read the 'Racing Post' everyday, studying form and his knowledge of the industry and the sport of racing is incredible.

Paddy got a job when he was just eleven in a racing yard. He has the gift. He did pony racing and learned all about the yard before he ever got on a race horse. He could do all the reign changes really fast and would go racing, leading up for his trainer Roger Ingram and his wife Sharon, who were wonderful and taught him all they knew about racing. Great people.

Paddy reading the Racing Post

Paddy's First Win

He rode out on the racing ponies' everyday
with their daughter, who is now a jockey also. Noel
used to take Paddy racing every month and even
when he was very young he would win lots of cash;
Paddy was very good at picking winners. Sometimes
Noel wouldn't listen to Paddy and instead would
follow his own instinct but Paddy was the only one
who would return home with a nice fat wallet!

Paddy left Roger and went back to Pat Phelan
who had a bigger yard. However, Pat couldn't take
him until he was sixteen years so he went to Brett
Johnson. Brett has been a big help to Paddy in

making his way and his wife was keen for Paddy to get his licence ASAP. Paddy then went for an interview at Jim Boyle's yard, the one next to Roger Ingram's. He would see the lads every day riding out and got to know them. It was a busy yard. He went for an interview to Jim Boyle who asked him why he had chosen his yard. Paddy spoke so well for himself; he said 'I've just turned sixteen; it's time I rode out some racehorses and started my career'.

Jim told Paddy his knowledge of racing was very good and that he was to come up and spend a whole day at the yard. 'I will watch you riding out and if I like what I see, I will ring you. I can't give you a job at the moment – I already have a jockey and I have enough staff in the yard. But I will ring some trainers for you to see if there's a place'. He could not have done fairer than that.

So, Paddy went and spent the day with Jim Boyle. He must have done something right when he was riding out, as when Paddy left to go home Jim shouted to him 'See you 6am Monday morning, don't be late!'

Noels brother John & Paddy

Newmarket Racing School and first winners!

Paddy stayed riding work at five in the morning and was soon going to go for his jockey licence. He met Pat Phelan lots of times and they got on well. He was always going back to work at Pats as it was Pat who, when he was younger, told Paddy to try Brett Johnson. So after a while he spoke to Jim about moving to Pat Phelan's. He just stayed until Jim's other work came back from Dubai and then he joined Pats yard.

Soon after that he went for his jockey licence. He never made a fuss and wouldn't let me see him ride until he finished Newmarket. When the day came Noel and I were like two excited kids as we climbed into a small van with a sliding door which was left open and his racing coach was beside the driver. She was lovely and was wearing a blue tooth ear piece. She told us Paddy was also wearing one.

My heart nearly jumped out of my chest as Paddy was told to go along side us; he was so still on this racehorse and he was talking to her all time. The she looked round and smiled at me and Noel, as if she knew what we were feeling. She said something to Paddy – go for it. The driver put the foot down, we were driving about 30 miles an hour and Paddy came galloping beside us.

The rail was so close to the van, she had left the sliding door open. Paddy took my breath away. Even Noel his Dad had water in his eyes. He knew that day, as I did, that the way Paddy looked – so neat and professional – that his career in racing had no boundaries.

The best day of my life since the two boys were borne was on Noel's birthday, on the second of December 2012. Paddy had his licence three months at that stage. He was 17 years old and he won on 'Representing Celtic' (No. 7) at Kempton in a photo finish. What a birthday that was! He had invited a few friends and his cousins in Ireland watched the race as well. His friends bought Noel a £50 wins on Paddy for his birthday. He then had a win Lingfield Park just three days later.

Paddy is humble about racing and doesn't talk about winning. Just how he wants to keep progressing as a jump jockey and to continue to work hard as his attitude is 'life is what you put into it'. But for me going racing is the part of my life with Noel that is the happiest.

Looking Back...Thinking forward

There are different kinds of alcoholics – but there are things we all have in common when it comes to quitting. Each one of us has to find something stronger than drink on which to build our lives away from the drink.

That's what made the difference in stopping, at least for me and Noel. That's the bridge over which we walked. I know there are a lot of other issues. The most important one is what Sr Consilio said to me: you have to accept the 'goodness of God' within you. That goodness – and knowing it's there – makes you able to accept, and change, whatever it is that needs changing. There is no point in looking to change other people. You have to find what it is that is causing the pain which you are trying to deny, and shut down even for a while and which is the reason for the drinking.

But you have to have a positive reason for stopping – something that will last. I mean, you might think that running the London Marathon or starting a business might make all the difference. But they won't keep doing it for you; you can't be running marathons all your life. To want to keep sober, it has to be something that will last. Kids last. Family lasts.

I often think of the promise me and Noel made to each other on that day I found out I was pregnant – that we would not take a drink until our child was at least twenty years old. Sticking to this promise really helped us stay sober.

I've often thought about what all of this means. In the end, people just have to admit to themselves that they have a drink problem; and a lot of people do not realise they have a drink problem until it's nearly too late. When you let go of your resentment and ask God to remove the desire to drink, then your addiction will begin to heal. Most alcoholics, if they can find or find themselves led to something on which to focus that has a higher value than drink, will also find what it is that will take them a long way from addiction. That, and help from compassionate professional people like Sr Consilio, sticking to the aftercare and AA meetings, and their own belief in God.

We gave up the drink to have kids. In our wildest dreams we never thought miracles could happen. But we are living proof of that they do happen when you take the first step and leave yourself open to miracles. We were told by professionals that two active alcoholics would never get sober, as one could fall of the wagon and the other would almost definitely follow suit. Perhaps that is true in general. But Noel and I did get sober and we never drank again. I am coming up to 60 years old and Noel is 65. We won't drink now – we have too much to live for, especially our two boys.

We have always been completely honest and open with our boys about our drinking – and our recovery. It was never 'a secret' or 'something that we don't talk about in front of the kids'. They just picked up on it.

When they were younger and into the teenage years, they noticed that when other kids parents suggested having a drink, or maybe going for a drink, we would be saying 'Thanks - but no thanks'. If they pushed it, we would be dead straight and just say that we were fully recovered from alcohol addiction and that we had no notion of going there again.

Both of our lads know that they were the reason we stopped. I think – they wouldn't say it – that they love us for that. So there has never been any old nonsense about the past. What's important for me and Noel is now – and their future. For sure, they love Sr Consilio who they visit every year for having accepted me as I was back in the day; who believed and taught me to believe that I was good and started me on the road from addiction to total recovery.

Journey's End

We were living in our home at Epsom for some time when we got a surprise! Living just around the corner from us was a family – the Skully's – from the 'Curragh' of Kildare. The Curragh is the great open countryside of Kildare, ideal for horse training and where some of the greatest champions have raced. Noel grew up only a few miles away, in Athy – and that was where Sr Consilio set up her first rehabilitation centre and where I met her for the first time: there has to be providence in these things!

Will & Paddy

Young Will Skully was playing on the same junior football team as Sean - the under 13 team – when they first met. Because he was that bit younger, they would bring on in the middle of the game and use him as what they called their 'secret weapon'.

Will's dad, Michael Skully, grew up on the Curragh. Michael is an ambulance driver and, as part of his job of being on call at big sporting events, has often tracked jockeys around the racecourse: it can be a dangerous sport and it's important to have a skilled ambulance crew available. Will is great friends with Paddy and Sean – they still love football – and remain friends to this day. He has his own key to our home to come and go as he pleases.

Paddy's other best mate is Dan Cremin. The two of them met at Jim Boyle's yard. Dan now races over the Flat for Mick Shannon. On his days off Paddy often drives to Lambourne to catch up with Dan. The two of them are always on the phone to each other and the banter between them is at times unmerciful. Dan came to see Paddy's first race at Plumpton, which I thought was really nice. It is great that both of our two boys have such good friends. I know only too well the difference that friendship makes to your life.

Dan Cremin

Paddy works long hours; early mornings and late nights and the preparations, the riding out and everything that goes with it is very demanding. But that's his profession – he loves it. He is full of self-belief and he has the ability to go right to the top. Paddy has always been good at calming down the younger horses. He looked after a horse called 'Jakey' from the time he was a two year old and he once calmed down 'Jakey' so much that he fell asleep in the stable near the Paddock. The jockey that was riding him that day looked at him and left him sleeping for as long as he dared! Jakey romped home first – and Paddy was absolutely over the moon. He had put so much into that horse. It's a great gift to have – that empathy with animals -- when you are working with horses.

At present, he is with Pat Phelan. Pat Phelan hasn't enough jump horses at the moment so he will probably be moving to a bigger yard in Lambourne later in July, before the season begins. Pat wants Paddy to move on and progress, but they will always be close friends; they had some great times at Ermyn Lodge stud, breaking in horses and driving all over the country to race meetings (including the winners circle, of course!)

Healing Hearts

I hope anyone reading this book that has a problem with addiction will get the grace to see that the challenges in committing to recovery are easy compared to the terrible sameness of waking up every day and finding yourself still stuck in addiction, preoccupied with the next drink or the next bet. Been there, done that. Noel and I found that special something that, for us, was much more important and fulfilling than all of that; and it was that which helped us take the big step towards recovery. And that was having our own family.

If anybody had told me back in the day that I would be driving my kids to football and racing. Picture it: walking into the racecourse with Paddy in his suit, his racing bag and whip sticking out of the bag, through the ticket office, pushed to the top of queue with no one saying a word to him. And then the women handing him the book, Paddy taking the pen and singing in his name and the name of the horse and trainer, saying: 'Oh, and I'll have a ticket for mum as well' and handing the ticket to me with a: 'I'll see you later mum' and off with him to the weighing room. The pride buzzing through me as he walked away and me thinking: 'Oh my God, he's Amazing!'

Let me say this to you, if you do have a drink problem: alcohol never, ever gave me the buzz I get from being my kids mum. God didn't just give me healthy kids, He gave me superstars. Sometimes I look at Sean and Paddy and think: 'how could anyone ever doubt that there is a God'.

And Noel, their father, the most genuine man I know on the planet; Noel, who shared my journey to recovery and with whom I now share my life. Noel and our kids fill my days. Art is important to me. Even as a child I loved art and it such a good feeling knowing that it is now a living part of my life. I sell some of my paintings in The Ebbisham Centre in Epsom.

My life experiences of identity, alienation and healing are among the themes that find their way into much of my work. As I write this, I am working towards an exhibition in Chelsea in the next year or two and praying the right opportunity comes along, from the right gallery, to exhibit my work. I know have total recovery; so can you, just let go, and let God take over.

Me, happy and healthy today.

Anne Bradley is an artist who has exhibitions of her work at The Ebbisham Centre, Epsom, Surrey.

Me and my father after I had recovered and come home

This book has been made possible by the generous support and sponsorship of Venford Construction Ltd.

9974334R00081

Printed in Great Britain
by Amazon.co.uk, Ltd.,
Marston Gate.